#ROFL

GW01453058

Hi. Liberty
Lovely to meet you!

HAHA

#LOL

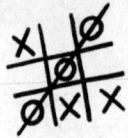

I would like to thank Ivor. If it wasn't for you by my side I would've been sat in a coffee shop telling myself jokes and the other customers would've thought I was weird.

Steven

To Steven, a brilliant writer and the funniest man in the world! (That is what you wanted me to say, isn't it, Steven?)

Ivor

HOW TO BE EVEN FUNNIER THAN THE FUNNIEST KID IN SCHOOL

IVOR BADDIEL & STEVEN VINACOUR

Illustrated by James Cottell

AWARD PUBLICATIONS LIMITED

ISBN 978-1-78270-653-3

Text copyright © 2025 Steven Vinacour & Ivor Baddiel

Illustrations by James Cottell
This edition copyright © Award Publications Limited

The rights of Steven Vinacour and Ivor Baddiel to be identified
as the authors of this work have been asserted in accordance
with the Copyright, Designs and Patents Act 1988.

All rights reserved. No part of this publication may be reproduced
or utilised in any form or by any means electronic or mechanical,
including photocopying, recording, or by any information storage
and retrieval system now known or hereafter invented, without
the prior written permission of the publisher.

First published 2025 by Award Publications Limited

Published by Award Publications Limited,
The Old Riding School, Welbeck,
Worksop, S80 3LR

 /awardpublications @award.books
www.awardpublications.co.uk

25-1165 1

Printed in the United Kingdom

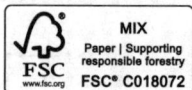

MIX
Paper | Supporting
responsible forestry
FSC
www.fsc.org
FSC® C018072

Award Publications Limited is not responsible and does not accept liability for the
availability or content of any website other than its own, or for any exposure to harmful,
offensive or inaccurate material that may appear on the Internet. Award Publications
Limited will have no liability for any damage or loss caused by viruses that may be
downloaded as a result of browsing the websites it recommends.

CONTENTS

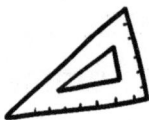

HOW TO BE EVEN FUNNIER

'How to be even funnier than the funniest kid in school.' It makes no sense, right? By definition, the funniest kid in school *is* the funniest kid in school (probably because they read our first book, **How to Be the Funniest Kid in School**, which is still very much available, if you haven't already read it). So, how can you be **FUNNIER** than them?

It's a conundrum, alright! And make no mistake, like all great conundra (if that's the plural of conundrum?), the answer (or answi — is that the plural of answer?), once you see it, is obvious. Being funny has **no limits**. It knows no bounds. It is like a great big wobbly jelly that keeps getting bigger, and therefore wobblier. It changes all the time.

So, what was the funniest gag in the world yesterday — 'Why was the parrot standing on a fish? It was a perch.' — is not the funniest gag in the world today. That's 'What is the friendliest sport to play? Nice Hockey.' And who knows what the funniest gag in the world will be tomorrow! (Unless you're reading this tomorrow, in which case you probably do know.)

Anyway, the point is, there's always more funny to be had. In fact, things could change at any moment, so you'd better not waste any more time. Start reading all the brand new gags in this book right away!

Go on, stop looking at us and get on with it...

SHOO!

Get out of here!

GO!

OK, now it's getting weird. We're leaving...

EXIT

THE ART OF JOKE TELLING

Before we go off to start work on *How to Be Even Funnier Than the Kid Who's Just Bought a Copy of How to Be Even Funnier Than the Funniest Kid in School*, a quick word about snorkelling...

That's for something else, Steven...

Is it? Well what is this bit about?...

There's a clue in the heading...

Ah yes, 'The Art of Joke Telling'...

It's a common mistake to think that when you tell a joke, you have to get a huge laugh and a big round of applause. In fact, there are a lot of reactions you can get that are just as acceptable, depending on the type of joke you decide to tell.

Reactions that are **GOOD** when you tell someone a joke:

Smiling

Grinning

ROFLing

LOLing followed by a ROFLing

LOLing

Snorting

HA HA

Laughing till head falls off

Reactions that are **NOT** so good when you tell someone a joke:

Puzzled staring

Yawning

Running away screaming

Crying

Parping

Falling asleep

You also have to take into consideration who you are telling the joke to. For instance, if you tell the joke below to someone who was born in the 1970s, they will fall off their chair laughing hysterically (unless they are not sitting on a chair). However, if you tell it to your school friends, they will look at you in complete confusion and then go and play with someone else. And, if you tell a baby they will say googoogaga and then probably poo their nappy.

Here is the joke:

Who sang 'Hive Talking'?
The Bumble Bee Gees!

HIVE
TALKIN'

Now, **YOU** might not understand that, but you have to trust us it's the best joke ever. Well, it's certainly the best joke ever that contains a song title and the name of a band who were popular in the 70s! So, the important thing is to work out if the person you are telling the joke to will understand the references in the joke. And maybe put a cushion on the floor next to the chair they are sitting on. If they are sitting on a chair, that is...

Happy joke telling!

LOL

HAHA

HAHA

ROFL

TOP TEACHERS

Teachers and headteachers are a funny lot. Not funny *ha-ha*, more funny *peculiar*, and some are funny *annoying*, funny *strict* or funny *boring*, or all four, which is not actually that funny at all, really. However, that most certainly does not rule them out as the subjects of jokes. Or is it the objects? I guess it's subjective. Or objective. Where was I?

Ah yes, the point is, that whether your teachers are funny or not doesn't really matter, because when you tell these jokes they, and everyone else, will be laughing their heads off. When this happens, they will be too busy looking for their head and will totally forget that you didn't do your homework. WIN-WIN!

Why did the teacher give the school principal a piggyback?

So people would say he had a good head on his shoulders.

Pupil 1: I'm in a dilemma. I have to go and see the school principal, but I also have a story to finish writing. I don't know what to do first?

Pupil 2: Flip a coin.

Pupil 1: Why?

Pupil 2: It's heads or tales!

Pupil: What years do you teach?

Teacher: Every year! I've been teaching since 1973.

Why did the school hire a cow?
To teach Moo-sic.

Why should schools have more
than one teacher in charge?
**Because two heads are
better than one!**

Which teacher does things
really quickly?
The head-faster.

What do you call the final
match of the school principals
tennis tournament?

The head to head.

What do you call someone
who's only ever worked in
an all boys school?

A teachim.

I told my PE teacher I was going to run a marathon.
She said I'd go far.

Where do teachers go when they feel sick?
The barf room!

What insect do you find in a classroom?
A teaching assist-ANT.

What subject do teachers teach
on the last day of term?
Bye-ology!

Why did the school hire a parrot?
To teach Pretty Polly-tics.

Why did the school hire a snake?
To teach Hiss-tory!

Pupil: Why did the class get a shock when the teacher came out of the stationery cupboard?

Teacher: She shouted, 'SUPPLIES!'

What do maths teachers eat?

Takeaways.

What can an art teacher draw but never paint?

The curtains!

Parent: Do you teach P.E. and I.T.?

English teacher: Yes, and all the other letters of the alphabet as well!

Why were the children only being taught about eyes, ears, nose, mouth, hair, cheeks, jaw and chin?

Because the lesson was being taken by the head teacher.

What does the geography teacher do if you misbehave in class?

Give you a sea-tention.

What does the home economics teacher do if you misbehave in class?

Give you a pea-tention.

I'M NOT HAP-PEA

BUZZZZTED!

DETENTION

What does the biology teacher do if you misbehave in class?

Give you a bee-tention!

What do you call the principal
of a zombie school?

The Deadteacher.

CLASSIC CORNER

What do you say to comfort
a grammar teacher?

They're, their, there.

Why did the teacher wear sunglasses?

Because his pupils were so bright!

They're certainly classics, Steven!

I know, that's why it's 'Classic Corner'.

But it's hardly a corner, is it?

No, but 'Classics Bottom of the
Page' doesn't quite have the same
ring to it.

HILARIOUS HOMEWORK

Taking schoolwork home?! What's all that about then? I mean, we don't take parts of our home to school! Otherwise I would definitely have taken the comfy chair from our lounge and my bed, which would've made school a lot more chill.

And what about your teddy bear?

I ASKED YOU NOT TO MENTION MY TEDDY BEAR, IVOR!

Sorry, Steven.

OK where was I? Oh yes, it's important to do homework for two very good reasons.

1) To stop us forgetting things and

2) ... I've forgotten what number two is.

You didn't do much homework at school then, did you, Steve?

No, I didn't. In fact, I still have some maths homework to hand in, it was due in 1982.

Wow, that's 27 years ago!

I can see you didn't do well in maths either.

Let's move on.

So, if you can't get out of doing your homework then you may as well have some fun with it. Which is why we've decided to write you some homework jokes and yes, we wrote these after school and the following day we handed them in. The teacher laughed so much that she wet herself. So, if you are about to read these rib-ticklers, have a spare pair of underpants ready just in case.

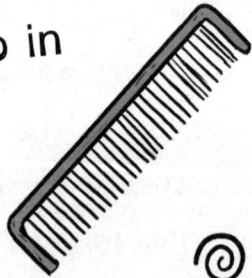

What do barbers do in the evenings?
Comb-work.

26

Pupil 1: I got an A for my homework.

Pupil 2: That's great!

Pupil 1: Not really. It was an, 'Eh? What on earth is this?'

EH?

Teacher: Why have you put a letter 'D' after the comma?

Pupil: I was practising my comedy!

What does Santa Claus do after school?

Ho Ho Homework.

Pupil: I'm sorry, Miss, but the dog ate my homework.

Teacher: Well that's bad news.

Pupil: Not really, he thought it was delicious and gave it an A+.

What sort of maths problems are Irish children best at?

Dublin!

Dad: Why are you dancing around the kitchen like that?

Daughter: I'm doing my home-twerk.

Pupil: I'm sorry, Miss, but the dog ate my homework.

English teacher: Is that the best excuse you can come up with?

Pupil: No, I'm saving my best one for the maths teacher.

Pupil 1: I got a B for my homework.

Pupil 2: That's pretty good.

Pupil 1: Not really, it stung me.

What should you do if you want to become a great detective?

Do your (Sherlock) Holmeswork.

What gets shorter the more you add?

Maths homework.

Why did the boy water the garden after school every day?

He was doing his hosework!

Pupil 1: Why have you changed your name to Late?

Pupil 2: So I don't have to do any homework.

Pupil 1: How come?

Pupil 1: Because the teacher always says, don't hand your homework in late.

Why did Spider-Man never get time to do his homework?

Because he spent too much time on the web!

CLASSIC CORNER

Pupil: Would you tell me off for something I haven't done?

Teacher: **Of course not.**

Pupil: Great, coz I haven't done my homework!

PLAYGROUND PUNS

Being funny in class has its risks, but when your classmates are bored out of their minds in a geography lesson or scratching their heads in maths, they are desperate for a laugh (or have nits). So, you could probably tell them the worst joke in the world and they would burst into hysterics. (The worst joke in the world, by the way, is 'Why did the chicken cross the road? To get to the other side.')

Being funny in the playground is a whole different kettle of fish, chips and ketchup, because that's where people are already having fun. They might already be laughing because Sanjiv stepped into a huge puddle during a game of hopscotch. Or because Lucy went to complain after Charley pushed her over and accidentally called the teacher 'Mum'.

A top jokester just sees this as a challenge though, with an added bonus of maybe winning whatever game it is they're playing. I mean, how difficult is it going to be to find someone in a game of hide-and-seek if you've shouted out a joke and they're laughing so hard that bogeys are flying out of their nose? And scoring a goal in football is going to be much easier if the goalkeeper is crying with laughter and can't see the ball because you've told a belter. So, march out into the playground and let loose with some of these rippers! You'll turn fun into funny and win every game you play without even trying.

What game are babies good at?
Footbawl!

Pupil 1: You're it.

Pupil 2: What is it?

Pupil 1: You are, you're it.

Pupil 2: I know, but what is it?

Pupil 1: You.

Pupil 2: Right, but what am I?

Pupil 1: It.

Pupil 2: How can I be it,
if I don't know what it is?

Pupil 1: Oh, I'm going to play
with someone else.

Why did my sister lose a game
of hide-and-seek to a wrestler?

Because John Cena.

What can pupils never
play at school?

Truant.

What do you get
if you cross a
playground game
with table tennis?

SkipPINGpong!

Why did the boy fall asleep
in the playground?

**He was playing with
a kipping rope.**

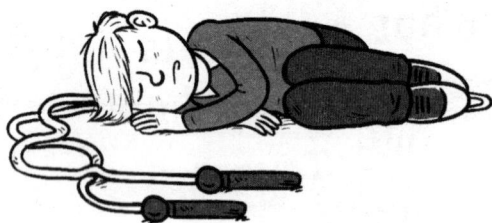

What game do the Muppets play?

Miss Piggy in the Middle.

Pupil 1: Why was the boy spinning
on his back in the playground?

Pupil 2: He was break-dancing!

Pupil 1: Why have you brought a fish to the playground?

Pupil 2: So we can play pat-a-hake.

Why did the pupils step towards the teacher whenever someone asked him what time it was?

His name was Mr Wolf!

What game can you play with a frozen pastry?

Iced pie.

What game always leaves the playground super clean?

Mop-scotch!

Why did the boy never come in from break?

He was playgrounded.

What do police officers play at school?

Cop-scotch!

Knock Knock

Who's there?

Wah.

Wahoo?

It's not that exciting.

Where do dogs go at breaktime?
To the playhound.

What is a toad's
favourite game?

Leapfrog!

What game do insects
love to play?

Bug-o-war.

Why did the chicken
cross the playground?

**To get to the
other slide!**

CLASSIC
CORNER

EXAM-ALAMADINGDONG!

OK, by now you are well on your way to being even funnier than the funniest kid in school. But, it's important that we test how much you are learning about joke writing and telling. Think of these as your G.C.S.Hehehes! Having read lots and lots of jokes, by now you will have worked out how to create a pun. Let us just recap the basic rules for you.

1. Take a word.

2. Take the first bit of the word or the second bit of the word and swap it for another word that rhymes.

3. Take a break (this joke writing stuff is exhausting).

4. Take a moment to work out the question leading up to the new word you've created.

5. Take a look for the perfect audience and then reveal your new joke.

6. Take a bow as they roll on the floor laughing.

Still not sure? Allow us to demonstrate! Take the word 'library'. Now, separate the word 'li' and 'brary' and start thinking about words that rhyme with each part. We thought of 'fly' for the first part and 'blurry' for the second part.

Now, create your new words — 'flybrary' and 'liblurry'!

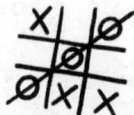

Then, add the question part of your new joke:

Where do insects go
to read books?
The Fly-brary.

Where do you go to read if
you can't find your glasses?
The Li-blurry.

Got it? I mean, you got it, but have you *got* it?
You have? OK, time to test you! All the following
jokes are based on well-known video games,
but can you guess the answers?

an
actual
ROFL

MEGA
LOLS

What game is played
on the beach?

Sandy Crush.

What Battle Royale game
is played by athletes?

Sport-nite.

What puzzle game do
pilots love to play?
Jetris.

What game do boys play?
Broblox.

What construction game must you play in silence?
Mime-craft.

What is the smelliest, grubbiest video game?
Grime-craft.

What game to ravens play?
Crowblox.

What building game is played
with cubes of bread?
Doughblox.

What football game
do giants play?

FeFiFoFum-Fa.

(We know FIFA has changed its name
now, but that's fine, it still works!)

What is a police officer's
favourite game?
Crime-craft.

What is a teacher's favourite
video game?
Taught-nite.

What game is full of mistakes?
Blooper Mario.

What game is good for
your pet cat's teeth?
Animal Flossing.

What puzzle game is
damp and soggy?

Wetris.

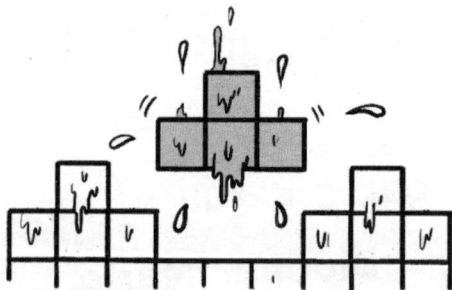

So, how did you do? Did you get them all right? You did? That's incredible! We got a few wrong and we wrote them. Well, congratulations! You've passed your G.C.S.Hehehes and you can now progress to Universiteeheeheee where we have lots more jokes for you. We even have some exam related jokes. Here goes...

What exams do you need to take if you want to make honey?
BEE-TECs!

Is a past paper
called an **ExExam?**

Is a past paper on Mexican cooking
called a **TexMexExExam?**

Is a past paper on Mexican
omelette cooking called a
TexMexEggsExExam?

What exams do
batteries take?

AA levels!

What exams do would-be
farmers take?

Hay levels.

What exams do you need to
take if you want to work
on the beach?

Bay levels.

Pupil 1: How did you get on in your spelling test?

Pupil 2: Terrably.

What tests do hens take?
Pexams.

Teacher: Why have you brought in your desk from home?

Pupil: You said you would be testing us on our tables today.

Why do teachers think
a game of football is
like exam papers?

**They both involve a lot
of marking.**

Why was the teacher
shouting questions at
the swimming pool?

**She was testing
the water.**

Pupil 1: How did you do in your History exam?

Pupil 2: Oh I'm not going to worry about it. It's all in the past!

Pupil 1: How was your Chemistry test?

Pupil 2: I was in my element.

Pupil 1: How did you do in your Geography exam?

Pupil 2: I was all over the place!

What should you do to make sure you do well in a football exam?

Pass.

Teacher: Did you answer all the exam questions?

Pupil: Yes, but I questioned all the answers.

And if you do have a test coming up, you best get revising! Try these books from the school library...

Top shelf:

WRITING JOKES by Izzy Funny

Starting to Write BY PAIGE ONE

Where Honey Comes From by B. BUM

Toilet Training Your Dog by Ivor Jessbin-Weedon

DON'T BE LATE! by Harry Up

Lost Property by Wes Mystuff

Cooking for Beginners by CHRIS P. CHIPS & TOM HART O'SAUCE

Bottom shelf:

UNLEASH YOUR CREATIVITY BY EMMA G. NATION

THE BORING FOOTBALL MATCH by ANIL NIL DRAW

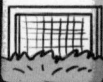

LEARN TO CARTWHEEL by JIM NASTICS

How to Put Up Big Tents by Mark E.

HA HA

TECHNO RULES

Where would we be without technology? Well, I'll tell you. I'd be right here, but there wouldn't be a computer in front of me. Instead, I'd be sitting facing the wall. I could write all the jokes on my wall and then invite you round to my house to read them, but that would take far too long and there are at least three of you that I don't want knowing where I live.

So, technology is very important, unless it stops working and then it's very important to find someone who knows how to make the technology work again. Ivor and I aren't very good with technology, but we are good at telling jokes that we've thought up to amuse the person that comes round and fixes all the things we break.

But let's take you back to the beginning (not

of this book, just of the world and stuff). Once upon a time, 'The Wheel' was thought of as a great technological advance. In fact, we have it on good authority that, back in 3000 B.C. (when it was updated to 'The Wheel 2.0'), people were falling over themselves to get hold of one... Though they'd probably need at least two. One wouldn't be much good unless you were a unicyclist, and there weren't many of those around back then.

Anyway, nowadays we must be on at least 'The Wheel 8506.0', and there have been loads of good jokes about wheels, such as...

Do you have wheels disease?

What's that?

I don't know but it's going round!

So, we don't really wheel... sorry... *feel* we should be doing jokes about 'The Wheel'.

Thankfully, though, there have been loads of other technological advances in recent times which *are* just ripe for joke-making — so ripe in fact that they are ready to be consumed. We *wheely* hope you enjoy them (sorry...)

What app do doctors and nurses use most?

SickTock.

My computer gives me a round of applause when I've completed my homework.

It's a claptop!

Who breaks into computers
whilst doing gymnastics?

A hack-robat.

What did Instagram do when
it won the race?

An app of honour.

Where do computer keyboards
go for a night out?

The Space Bar!

Where do you find
information about
ducks?

On a webbed-site.

What is a crocodile's
favourite app?

Snapchat!

Did you hear about the boy
who played his video game
on an escalator?

**He wanted to get to
the next level.**

Why are computer programs
like comfy slippers?

They're both soft wear.

What's the best way to send someone a joke?

By hehehe-mail!

O	HE HE HE	😊
O		✉
O		✉

What app do older women prefer?

Instagran... and they also like nan-otechnology.

Why did the girl have female horses in her ears?

She was wearing MarePods.

Why did the climber take his computer up a mountain?

He wanted to get into a high-tech career!

Where should you store information about anoraks?

In a zip file.

Why did Sir Isaac Newton dislike computers?

Because when the Apple fell on his head, it really hurt!

What does someone with a very big mouth have in common with a computer?

Megabytes.

What is the study of broken computers called?

Wrecknology!

What new technology can see things very clearly?

A eye.

What is it called when a spy make up information?

Artificial intelligence.

CLASSIC CORNER

Why did the computer get cold?

Its windows were left open!

Why did the computer break up with the internet?

There was just no connection.

SPORTS DAY

What could be better than a whole afternoon set aside to run around, play games and not do any real lessons? It's perfect! Unless it rains, or snows, or is too hot, or too cold, or the games are too complicated, or you fall over, or you are so busy waving at your parents while you run that you bump into your friend and both fall over, or a swarm of a million bees fly in and—

Ok, I think that's enough. Sports day is great and if we can refer you back to the section on playground games, you'll know that to guarantee a win, all you have to do is tell a couple of these awesome jokes to the people you are competing against! They will be so busy rolling on the floor whilst crying with laughter, that you will run straight past them and win the egg and spoon race!

Or the sack race!

Or the three-legged race!

Or the three-legged egg and spoon sack race!

Unless, that is, the event you are taking part in involves having to roll around on the floor in hysterics, in which case they might win. So, check the rules first, which is actually good advice for any event you're taking part in. I once turned up to the egg and spoon race with a very slippery fried egg and — surprise, surprise — I didn't win. I did enjoy quite a nice breakfast, though.

Where do school children in Helsinki run to in a race?
The Finnish line!

Who is the worst sports teacher?

Mr Goal.

When is the best time to visit the Wimbledon tournament?

Ten-ish.

What martial art would you wear a bright orange suit for?

Carottee!

Pupil 1: I do martial arts –
the ancient sport of judo.

Pupil 2: Judon't.

Pupil 1: I do!

Which martial art does the
royal family do?

King Fu.

What is a ghost's
favourite martial art?

Kung BOO!

What American sporting
event is held in a toilet?

The Pooper Bowl!

What do computer geeks do
in the swimming pool?

Hack stroke.

What is a wild animal's
favourite way to swim?

Beast stroke!

Which sport does the
church choir excel at?

Hymnastics!

What is the best exercise
to do after eating too
many crisps?

Crunches.

Which animals are best at
playing rounders?

Bats!

What is the best
exercise to do in a lift?

Press-ups.

Why do eggs rarely win races?
Because they're often beaten.

What is the best exercise
to do after eating too much
guacamole and hummus?

Dips!

What race do maths
teachers like best?
The 4 x 100 metres relay.

What event do burglars take
part in on sports day?

The ROBstacle race!

What's the smelliest
sports day event?

The pong jump!

What race do astronauts run?

The 100 meteors.

What's the best cake to eat
before a relay race?

Baton-burg.

What do you call a female
P.E. teacher who can't
score a goal?

Miss!

What event do people who
borrow money take part in?

A repay race.

What sports day event do
they play in space?

The egg and moon race.

Why was the oak tied
to the sycamore?

**They were in the
tree-legged race.**

What contest did everyone
fall asleep in?

Tug-o-snore!

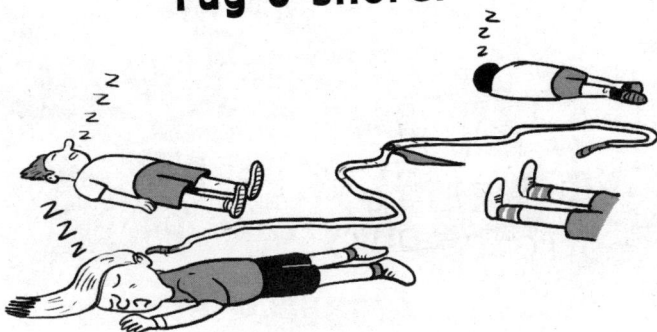

What advice should you give
to your competitors before
a 100 metre race?

It's a marathon not a sprint.

Teacher: We have a new sports event this year children. We're going to go fishing in the school pond!

Pupil: But how do we know who wins?

Teacher: It's whoever gets first plaice.

CLASSIC CORNER

Why did the golfer wear two pairs of trousers?

In case he got a hole in one!

PURRFECT PETS

Pets are great! They play, cuddle, get us to take exercise and we can blame them when we do a really stinky parp.

If you are *very* lucky, you might have a class pet or a school pet. Our teacher at school once said she was going to get a class pet, and she was thinking of getting a skunk. We said, 'What about the smell?' and she replied, 'I'm sure it will get used to you eventually.' Rude!

Anyway, pets are naturally funny. Think of a tortoise on a trampoline or a hamster in a leotard or just the dog breed Schnoodle and you'll laugh (which is good)! However, they are terrible at telling jokes and not very good at listening to them either (which is bad). Whenever I try to tell my dog a 'Knock, knock,' joke, he starts barking and runs to the front door. He never even asks me who's there.

Therefore, we suggest only telling these jokes to people who have pets, rather than the pets themselves. Because the chances of seeing a lurcher laugh, a goat giggle or a chimp chuckle are very slim indeed.

What do frogs wear on their feet?
Open-toad sandals.

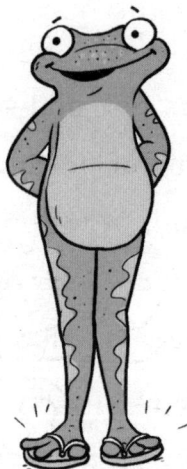

What do you give a sick horse?
Cough stirrup.

What breed of dog performs magic?

A Labracadabrador.

What does it take to make an octopus laugh?

Ten tickles!

HEE HEE

Feather duster

Which breed of dog must you say hello to when in Japan?

A Konnichihuahua.

What children's song do mice like to sing?

Heads, Shoulders, Cheese and Toes.

What do you get if you cross a chicken and a dog?

A Cock-a-poodle-doo!

Where do sheep go to meet up for something to drink?

A coffee baa.

What fast food do rabbits eat?
Hoppy meals.

Why is a giraffe like
a storybook?

They both have tall tails.

Which football team do
tailless cats support?

Manxchester United.

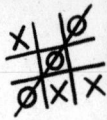

Why couldn't the turtle get any money out of the cash machine?

She'd forgotten her terrapin number.

Pupil 1: You see that dog over there?

Pupil 2: The one wearing glasses?

Pupil 1: Yes.

Pupil 2: What about him?

Pupil 1: His bark is worse than his sight.

Why are snails so shy?

Because they rarely come out of their shells.

Which dogs are best at drawing?

Labradoodles!

Which animal is brown, jumps up and down, and smells terrible?

A kangapoo.

What do you call a well-dressed cat in a taxi?

A fabby-looking tabby in a cabby.

How can you tell the difference between an African elephant and an Indian elephant?

Ask them where they're from.

What language do birds speak?
Pigeon English.

What do you get when you cross a frying pan and a popular pet?

A non-stick insect!

Where do dogs go to catch a train?
The Alstation.

What do snakes do when
they're in a bad mood?

They have a hissy fit.

What sort of snake is good
at cutting grass?

A mower constrictor!

What snakes are useful if
you're driving in the rain?

Windscreen vipers.

How do birds prepare for exams?
They learn things parrot fashion.

Pupil 1: It's my pet bird's birthday today.

Pupil 2: Send him my budgerigards.

Why do bunnies never stop talking?
Because they keep rabbiting on.

Pupil 1: I took my pets out last night in the mist and rain.

Pupil 2: What happened?

Pupil 1: My moggy and doggy got soggy in the foggy.

What has a trunk, two wheels
and a horn? ✳

An elephant on a motorbike

Why is your lizard so small?
Because it's my newt!

My dog's got no nose!
How does it smell?
Awful!

WEATHER, WHATEVA!

Having to stay in the classroom because it's raining is called 'wet play', which is bonkers because the point of keeping you inside is so you don't get wet! It should really be called 'dry play'. Unless you live in Germany where drei (pronounced 'dry') is the word for three. That means you would get three playtimes! We should all move to Germany in my opinion.

That's very interesting, Steven, but isn't the weather 'wetter' in Germany?

I've no idea Ivor and, to be honest, I've kind of moved on to the jokes now... If you want to learn a new language you'll have to do it in your own time and not when we are busy with the serious business of joke telling.

Gut, danke, gutentag.

What does that mean, Ivor?

It means get on with the jokes,
Steven, and stop messing around!

What type of weather is
the most visible?

I see!

Why do babies usually
play indoors?

**Because they're often
wet and windy.**

Why is it always wet outside
when a king or queen
visits a school?

Because they're reigning.

I was eating a bowl
of soup in the
playground and it
started raining.

**It took me four
hours to finish
my lunch!**

In which country do sheep fall from the sky?

Bahrain.

✳ Why were their lots of animals in the playground?

They thought it was vet play!

FRENZ AND FAM, INNIT!

They say you can choose your friends, but you can't choose your family. But we have no idea who 'they' are, and what about family friends?

Can you choose them? Clearly, whoever 'they' are, 'they' have no idea what 'they' are talking about,

unlike us. We know that if you choose to tell these jokes, your friends and your family will be lolling like they've just entered a lollathon (that might not actually exist, but it really should).

Anyway, if you do tell them, you will definitely be chosen as the funniest friend or family member of all time — much funnier than all your other friends, as well as Uncle Norman, Aunty Doris and Pablo Suarez, your third cousin six times removed who you've never met and didn't know about until just now.

Why were all the relatives gluing pictures into a scrapbook?
Because families stick together.

What do you call your brother or sister when they get dressed up in loads of sequins and sparkly stuff?

Your si-bling!

What do you call a relative you aren't that bothered about?

Meh-phew.

Which relative is always letting people in and out of rooms?

Door-ter.

Why is your Auntie June married to the least trendy member of your family?

He's OK really. He can't help it if he's Uncool Pete!

Which family member is good at keeping secrets?

Your mother, because she's best at keeping mum.

I live in England, my cousin lives in Australia.

He's a distant relative.

What does your uncle's wife like to drink?

Arn-tea.

What is a good song to sing to your siblings's daughter?

Heads, Shoulders, Niece and Toes.

What ships never sink?

Friendships.

What camera does an action-packed brother use?

A Go-bro!

How does your closest relation read books?

On a next of kin-dle.

How do farmers pay for their online shopping?

HayPal.

What do birds call their oldest mates?

Their nest friends.

Why are birds always so successful?

Because they have friends in high places.

CLASSIC CORNER

How did Darth Vader know what he was getting for Father's day?

He felt Luke's presents.

SICK NOTES

The worst thing about being sick is not feeling well. On the other hand, if someone describes you as 'well sick', that's good. It's confusing and complicated and, thinking about it, it might make you feel bad, which is bad. Unless it's bad meaning good, which is good.

Anyway, where was I? Oh yes, the good thing about having a sick day is you get to stay in bed, maybe watch TV and have someone bring you soup if you're lucky. Unless you don't like soup, in which case you can give it to Ivor and I as we both like soup. So, here are our jokes about soup...

Who has the catchphrase – 'Is it a bird, is it a plane, is it leek and potato?'

Souperman!

Ummm hang on a minute, Steven, why are you doing jokes about soup?

Well Ivor, I thought this chapter was about soup? We could include other starters, like garlic bread, garlic bread with cheese and garlic bread with cheese and tomatoes.

STEVEN! STOP TALKING ABOUT STARTERS! THIS IS A JOKE BOOK ABOUT SCHOOL! YOU ARE SUPPOSED TO BE WRITING ABOUT SICK DAYS!

School? Right, well that does make more sense to be honest Ivor. I don't know why you'd write a chapter about garlic bread and soup. Fine, OK, here are some jokes about being off sick. If I were you, Ivor, I'd give up on the whole soup and garlic bread idea to be honest.

AARRRGGGGHHHHH!!!

Patient: Doctor, doctor! I'm addicted to social media.

Doctor: I don't follow.

Patient: Doctor, I keep eating hay and galloping about.

Doctor: You need a horsepital.

What is the best way to avoid music lessons?

Ask your parents to write a note.

Patient: Doctor, whenever I get measured for a suit I can't stop singing pop songs.

Doctor: Taylor Swift?

Patient: Yes, he's pretty quick. But, I still manage to get through a verse or two!

What's runny and always smells?
Your nose.

Why is cricket like diarrhoea?

Both of them involve getting the runs.

Doctor, doctor!
I feel like an app.

Well, take this tablet...

How does it feel if you hurt yourself in Madrid?

It's very Spainful.

Patient: Doctor, I think I caught a virus on the way over here.

Doctor: Flu?

Patient: No, I came by bus.

What's the worst excuse a young leopard can give for not going to school?

I'm covered in spots!

What can you lose but never tell anyone?

Your voice.

Why did the
waste bin take
a day off?

It felt rubbish.

Doctor, doctor! I feel like
a board game.

**My advice is to go straight
home, do not pass 'Go',
do not collect £200.**

Pupil: I'm sorry I can't come
in today, I feel pony.

Teacher: What do you mean?

Pupil: I'm a little hoarse.

Why couldn't the driving instructor take his students for their lessons?

He had gear-ache.

Why did the young bee not go to school?

He had a bad honey-ache.

Why was the baker's daughter not in school?

She had a bread-ache.

Why was the school principal off for the day?

He had a head-ache.

What illness do pilots
always get?

Flu.

Where do divers go if they
have an accident?

A & Sea.

Teacher: Are you sure your
mother wrote this sick note?

Pupil: Oh yes, why do you ask?

Teacher: Because it says
'Please can my son be excused
from P.E. today as he has
chicken socks'.

Teacher: This note says you have to leave school early today to go to the dentist for a filling. Is that correct?

Pupil: Yes, Miss. It's the tooth, the whole tooth and nothing but the tooth!

How do train drivers sneeze?

Achoo-choo!

Teacher: I heard you were making naughty words out of your alphabetti spaghetti at lunch today, and now you say you're not feeling well.

Pupil: Yes, I think I've got rude poisoning...

CLASSIC CORNER

Why don't ants get sick?
Because they have anty-bodies!

SCHOOL'S OUT FOR SUMMER

Half-term, summer break, they are great, aren't they? They're just like taking a holiday from school...

That's exactly what they are, Steven. That's why they are called school holidays...

Well, anyway, they give you the opportunity to play with your friends, take some day trips, even maybe go on an actual holiday. And best of all, you don't have to think about school. All you have to think about is how much fun you can have and how much ice cream you can eat.

But, in between (or even during), having fun and eating ice cream, there is nothing better

than dropping in a well-timed joke and claiming the title of funniest person on holiday. Or saying something so funny your friends laugh so hard that ice cream comes out of their noses.

What is your obsession with ice cream?

I just *really* want an ice cream.

Well, finish writing this bit, Steven, and then you can have one!

The end.

Is that OK, Ivor?

I suppose so...

Where's the funniest place
to go on holiday?
Costa del LOL.

What is a pilot's favourite
ice cream flavour?
Plane vanilla.

What's the worst kind of
day off school?
A rank holiday.

Dad: How are you enjoying our holiday seeing wild animals in Africa?

Son: Safari so good!

click!

Why is half-term like fracturing your finger?

They're both small breaks!

Teacher: Did you see any ancient ruins on your holiday?

Pupil: Only my parents.

Why is Santa's transport so cool?
Because it sleighs.

What should you give Father Christmas when he is finished delivering presents?

A round of Santapplause.

Why didn't Santa buy a few more animals to pull his sleigh?

Because they were too dear.

When do wild animals
take a holiday?

Beaster.

What do comedians
take on holiday?

Pun cream!

PUN
CREAM

Pupil 1: My friend asked
me if my birthday was
in the summertime.

Pupil 2: July?

Pupil 1: No, I told the truth.

Teacher: Did you fly overseas this summer?

Pupil: No, we took a submarine and went underseas!

Pupil: I went on a camping holiday.

Teacher: How was it?

Pupil: Intense.

What make of car would you find in the zoo gift shop?

A toy otter!

How do you describe a beach
using only two letters?

S and Y.

Where do roosters sit
on an aeroplane?

In the cock-a-doodle-do-pit.

Why did the boy
take a bucket and
spade up a tree?

It was a beech.

Why was the hotel like a
very small galaxy?

It had five stars.

In case you're thinking, 'What? holidays don't
have anything to do with school?', holidays *are*
part of school. If you didn't go to school, you
wouldn't be able to have a holiday from school,
so even though this book is about being funny
in school, this chapter is allowed and that
is our final word on the matter.
Until the next word. Or words.

AFTER-SCHOOL CLUBS

When the bell rings there is no better feeling
than knowing you can put down your books and
enjoy an after-school club (unless your after-
school club involves picking up books in which
case, put down some books and pick up other
books... or something). It's a time to learn a
new skill, get creative, or run around getting all
sweaty and stinky.

Er... Steven, running around getting sweaty and
stinky isn't an actual club.

Well, it was in my school, Ivor, and I got
a trophy for it! Well, I would've been given a
trophy but the teacher didn't want to get close
enough to give it to me. But it still counts.

So, from sports to stamp collecting, and from

making to baking, whatever you chose to do after school, make sure you include a gag or two to show that even after the bell rings you are still the king or queen of comedy.

What is trampolining club like?
It has its ups and downs.

Teacher: Welcome to drama club! Today we are going to act out a play I've written. It's about a giant monkey who rings your doorbell and in a happy, melodic voice asks you if you want to go and play table tennis. It's called **Ding Dong, King Kong, Sing Song, Ping Pong!**

Why does it take ages to get into the snooker club?

Because there is always a cue!

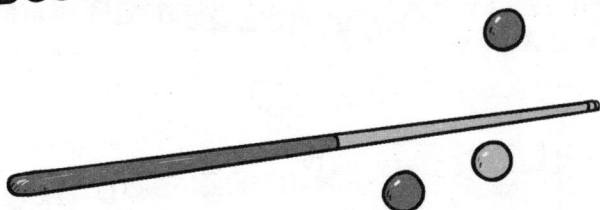

"Yo, bro, what time does Chess Club start?"

"No idea. Let me check, mate."

Why is rowing so popular?

Because it's oarsome!

Why did the pupils in
Computer Club keep
falling asleep?

Because they needed an app.

In Drama Club, what is it
called when the boys make it
up as they go along?

Himprovisation.

How does a bowler hurt
their neck?

They crick it.

LOST PROPERTY

(Stuff we couldn't fit in elsewhere!)

This is a curious mix of categories, but it is absolutely definitely not because we didn't have enough jokes to make each one a separate section, so decided to lump them all in together, is it, Steve?

Erm, no, it absolutely definitely isn't, Ivor, so why don't you tell everyone why we did put them all together?

Oh, well, I thought you could do that, Steve?

Really? But you're much better at explaining things like that.

I know, but that's exactly why you should do it, to get better at it... Steve? Steve? Where have you gone? Oh dear, I'd better see what's happened to him, he might have fallen down a

hole or been eaten by a giant worm,
or slipped into a parallel universe.
Probably best if you just enjoy the
jokes in the meantime.
Steve, hold on,
I'm on my way...

yum

UNIFORMS

What do young frogs
wear to school?

Jumpers.

What do firefighters'
children wear to school?

Blazers.

Why did the football coach
get thrown out of school?
They didn't allow trainers.

Why did the shirt get shirty?
Because the tie got tied up.

What do Bart and Lisa
Simpson wear for school?
Cartooniform.

How do you tell
footwear to
go away?
Shoo!

Teacher: Why are you wearing swimming trunks?

Pupil: I thought we had to wear pool uniform.

Why was the final score of the football match like part of the school uniform?

Because it was a tie.

Why were all the pupils dressed up as the same mythical creature?

They were wearing the school unicorn.

ASSEMBLIES, PLAYS AND WINTER CONCERTS

What do you call a rap about the forest?

Poet-tree.

Teacher: I want you all to bring in your windows tomorrow.

Pupil: Why?

Teacher: Because it's our turn to do glass assembly.

What do you call the tasty food you get at the end of year disco?

Prom nom nom nom nom.

Why couldn't the ghost perform in the school play?

It gave everyone stage fright.

Why did the dog audition for the school play?

He wanted the lead role.

Why did the class dress up as felines for the Christmas performance?

They were doing a cativity play.

Why is it important to perform Hamlet, Macbeth and A Midsummer Night's Dream?

They're good Shakesperiences.

What do donkeys have every day in school?

Ass-embly!

SNACK TIME

What did the salad say when
it couldn't get out of the
escape room?

Lettuce leaf.

What is an influencer's
favourite dessert?

TickyTocky pudding.

What's a Star Wars character's
favourite vegetable?

Ewokoli.

What do you get
if you cross Lego
with a vegetable?

Blockoli.

What kind of person
doesn't like bread?

A weirdough.

Where do monks like
to go for lunch?

Nundo's.

What did the sushi say
to the bee?

Wasabi?

BONUS SECTION

Well done for getting this far! Now you are officially funnier than the funniest kid in school! In fact, you deserve a reward, so we are presenting you with... the Bonus Section!

This section is stuffed with jokes that have nothing to do with school, but they are too funny not to share. After all, the funniest kids are funny EVERYWHERE, not just at school. After all, the funniest kids are always on the lookout for laughs!

Knock, knock.

Who's there?

Deliver.

Deliver who?

Oh, great – my takeaway! I'm starving!

Old MacDonald sold his farm and opened up a VR tech company called 'A-I-A-I-O'.

What happens if you invite a magician to your birthday party?

They bring lots of cards, but you only get to pick one!

What rank in the army is the most secretive?

Private.

What part of a vehicle is the sleepiest?

The wheels, because they are always tyre-d.

What is yellow, tasty and really politically correct?

Egg woke.

What time of day needs repairing?

Dawn – it's always breaking!

What are the fittest
sea creatures?

Mussels.

Why was each contestant
on a quiz show given a
bird of prey?

**For the fingers-on-the-
buzzards round.**

What month never
stops moving?

March.

How many very religious
women does it take to
change a light bulb?

Nun.

What is the handiest
thing you can shake?

A hand.

What's leafy, green and edgy?

An 'edge.

What household chore
always sucks?

Vacuum cleaning.

What animal loves rap music?

A hip-hop-potamus.

What do Australian kids
play with on rainy days?

A koalaring book.

Where would you find diamonds
that belong to me?

A mine.

How does the railway
get in shape?

It trains.

What can you pick
but not choose?

Your nose!

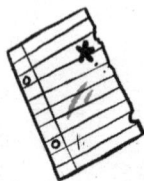

Pupil 1: What's all that
wailing and crying coming
from the plum tree?

Pupil 2: It's a damson in
distress.

What do hammers say after they've done a particularly good job?

Nailed it!

What cars to cowboys drive?
Audi, partner.

What type of paper always wipes clean?

Toilet paper.

What do you call a
bumblebee with
no bottom?

A blebee.

How do you tell a
shirt to shut up?

Button it!

What happened to the snake
that disappeared?

**No one knows –
it's a bit of a hisstery.**

What jokes are Italian
chefs best at telling?

Gnocchi, gnocchi jokes.

What is a knight's favourite
TV show?

Strictly Come Lancing.

Did you know that there
are lavatories for sale now
in the garden centre?

**They've started selling
toilet-trees.**

What do fish like to listen to?

Codcasts.

What do bricklayers like
to listen to?

Hodcasts.

What do people who go fishing
like to listen to?

Rodcasts.

What's the best day of the
week to wear a baseball cap?

Haturday.

How does a captain of a ship keep an eye on everything?

They use see sea TV.

(Oh, you like that one? Well how about...)

What do the Spanish police use to keep an eye on everything?

SÍ SÍ TV.

What TV show do birds of prey like to watch?

Britain's Got Talons!

Missed out on being the funniest kid? Grab it NOW!

ISBN: 978-1-78270-533-8

STEVEN VINACOUR

Steven started his comedy career about 600 years ago as a jester for Henry VIII. He entered a new talent show, 'Tudor You Think You Are?', but came second to someone juggling bagpipes!

He can often be heard shouting 'knock knock', but usually only after his family have locked him out for telling too many jokes. He has been voted the world's funniest writer 136 times (by his mum).

He now sits alone and writes the **Ted and His Time-Travelling Toilet** series, occasionally surfacing to run an award-winning production company, writing and directing commercials.

IVOR BADDIEL

Ivor has wanted to write jokes since he was 10 years old. That was when he broke his foot and received a letter addressed to 'I've A Bad Heel'. He laughed his head off, which, with a broken foot as well, meant he was in a bad way, but he soon recovered.

Since then, he's written jokes for lots of TV shows and quite a few books, and thinks that if you get this book, you won't be saying, 'I've a bad deal,' you'll be saying, 'I've a very good deal.'

ALSO BY STEVEN VINACOUR...

ISBN 978-1-78270-384-6

ISBN 978-1-78270-385-3

Don't miss Ted's *AMAZING*
TIME-TRAVELLING TOILET
ADVENTURES!

ISBN 978-1-78270-473-7

ISBN 978-1-78270-479-9

ISBN 978-1-78270-476-8

TED AND HIS TIME-TRAVELLING TOILET

ROMAN REWIND

Turn the page for a **sneak preview** of *TED'S* whacky and wonderful world of **TOILET TIME-TRAVELLING**. One flush and you're **away**!

WARNING:
CONTAINS TOILET HUMOUR!

YOU →

CHAPTER 1

I'm Ted and I have a **secret**. Actually, I have two secrets. The first one is just a normal, ordinary secretive kind of secret. The other, on the scale of secrets, with one being a teeny, tiny little secret and ten being the most **humungous**, jaw-dropping, **pant-wettingly** enormous secret — this is definitely a ten... and a bit.

If I were to come straight out and just tell you the secret then it's possible that the shock of hearing it could cause your head to pop off your shoulders like a cork from a bottle. I would feel very guilty if that happened to you and I'd have to answer very ANGRY emails from your parents telling me that I caused your head to pop off, fly out the window, land on a passing lorry and be carried off never to be seen again. No one wants that.

So, I'll start by telling you the little secret first and we will just have to see how well you cope. First you have to promise never to tell anyone...

... promise?

... really promise?

... really, really, really promise?

OK, I'll tell you. Come a bit closer ...

... closer ...

... even closer ...

THAT'S TOO CLOSE!

Back up a bit.

Too far ...

Take half a step forward ...

Hmmm... take a quarter of a step

backwards.

There... stop... OK. Now, before I tell you, you also have to promise that you won't laugh. You won't, will you? And when I say laugh I also mean **giggle**, chuckle, **chortle**, cackle, snigger, smile, **guffaw** and titter.

All right then. Ready?

Shhhhh...

Here goes...

My name isn't really Ted!

I know, right? **Mind blowing!**

Let me explain.

I re-named myself Ted as soon as I turned ten. I decided on Ted because it was the shortest name I could possibly think of which was the exact opposite of my real name which, thanks to my parents, is the stupidest, most ridiculously long name in the whole entire world. They decided to name me the most stupidest, longest, most ridiculously long name in the **whole entire world** because they thought it would give me character. In fact, all it gave me was a sore hand whenever I wrote my name on my homework! So, if you promise not to laugh I will tell you my full name ...

... promise?

Really, really, truly, hand-on-heart promise?

OK, here goes...

My full name is Terry Barry Larry Gary Harry Jerry Perry Lenny Benny Johnny Tommy Julie Jones.

Are you laughing? Because you promised not to.

The problem is that my parents are hopeless at making decisions. Some nights they spend so long making up their minds what they want for supper that it's time for breakfast. So, when my mum was pregnant with me, they made a list of all the names they liked and then couldn't decide which one to give me, so they gave them all to me. At that time, they also didn't know if I was going to be a girl or a boy. If I turned out to be a girl, I would've just been named Julie as that is the only girl's name they liked. When I turned out to be a boy they felt it was a shame to waste such a lovely name (bleugh) and so they put it on the end. Typical isn't it? The only quick decision they ever made and it was the wrong one!

The last time I heard my full name was when I got myself into trouble for 'accidentally' repainting my school trousers. Grey is such a boring colour and I thought green stripes would work this season. When I noticed that I'd also managed to get green paint all over my bed sheets, I knew I'd be in double trouble. So, when my mum stood at the bottom of the stairs with her hands on her hips and shouted, 'Terry Barry Larry Gary Harry Jerry Perry Benny Johnny Tommy Julie Jones, come down here at once!' I knew what was coming.

I didn't move. She called again and again. Finally, she marched up the stairs and burst in through my door knocking over a pile of comics I'd just sorted out.

'Why didn't you answer me when I called?' she shouted.

I pointed out her mistake at once.

'You missed out Lenny.'

'What?' she replied.

'You missed out Lenny. My name is Terry Barry Larry Gary Harry Jerry Perry Lenny Benny Johnny Tommy Julie Jones, and <u>you</u> said Terry Barry Larry Gary Harry Jerry Perry Benny Johnny Tommy Julie Jones, which technically isn't my name so I couldn't be sure that it was me you were calling.'

Mum stood in the doorway counting out

my names on her fingers. I waited for her
to realise that she had made the mistake. I
went back to reading my comic until she had
figured it out.

'Right, well anyway... <u>You</u> are in big trouble,
young man. What on earth were you thinking?
Painting your school trousers with green
stripes? And you've ruined your bed sheets!'

'I was being creative, Mum. I was thinking
outside the box.'

'What box?' asked Mum.

'<u>The</u> box, not <u>a</u> box,' I explained. Mum
scratched her head and looked confused.

'You don't have a box.'

'I know, but if I did... ' I replied.

'But you don't!' she argued.

'BUT IF I DID!'

'How big is it? Where would you keep it?
Your room is full of junk. Put the junk in the
box.'

'What box?' I asked.

'The box?' she said.
'What box?'

Now we were both confused about the box that we don't have, and Mum had completely forgotten why she came upstairs in the first place so I avoided getting told off about the green striped school trousers.

Now, let's move on to the second secret. This is the big one. And when I say big, I mean

BIG!

In order for me to tell you, we are going to have to go somewhere completely safe where no one could possibly hear what I say. I was thinking under my bed or in my wardrobe, but if Mum comes in again and finds me hiding in my wardrobe or under my bed with a complete stranger, then questions are going to be asked. So, there is only one option left. You take this book somewhere quiet and double-check that no one is listening then I'll tell you.

It's OK, I'll wait...

Ready?

Double-check again that no one is listening.
Just in case. OK, here goes... I have a
TIME-TRAVELLING toilet!

Shhhh!

Don't say anything. Just let the **pant-dropping awesomeness** of what
I just told you sink in slowly and then I'll tell
you all about it in a little while.

Sit down, calm down, maybe even go to the
toilet. You know, your normal, ordinary
non-time-travelling toilet. Unlike mine which is
time-travelling.

Did I mention that?

Oh no, you've become all excited again.

Sit down (again). Calm down (again).

I'll be back in a minute...

#ROFL

Haha

HAHA

#LOL